Original title:
Winter Bloom

Copyright © 2024 Swan Charm
All rights reserved.

Author: Daisy Dewi
ISBN HARDBACK: 978-9916-79-990-1
ISBN PAPERBACK: 978-9916-79-991-8
ISBN EBOOK: 978-9916-79-992-5

A Snowflake's Kiss

A whisper from the sky, so fair,
Delicate touch, beyond compare.
Dancing down with silent grace,
A snowflake's kiss, a soft embrace.

Beneath the twilight's gentle glow,
A world transformed, as breezes flow.
Each flake a story, pure and bright,
Painting dreams in purest white.

Cold Light, Warm Heart

In winter's chill, the stars do shine,
Casting shadows, soft and fine.
Yet in the heart, a spark ignites,
A warm embrace on frosted nights.

Through icy winds, the hope does soar,
In every heart, there lies a core.
With laughter shared, the cold retreats,
Warmth blooms where love and friendship meets.

Blossom Beneath the Drifts

Beneath the white, the echoes lie,
Whispers of blooms where dreams can fly.
Snowdrops peep through winter's hand,
A sign of spring in dormant land.

Amidst the drifts, life takes its pause,
Nurtured by nature's silent laws.
With patience held, the sun will break,
And life will rise from winter's wake.

Secrets in the Snow

In pristine fields where stillness reigns,
The snow conceals, what it retains.
Footprints whisper tales untold,
Of secrets kept in glistening gold.

As shadows stretch and daylight wanes,
Underneath the snow, the mystery reigns.
Each flake a keeper of a tale,
Of winter nights and moonlight pale.

Cold Nights

The moon hangs low, a silver eye,
Whispers of wind, a soft goodbye.
Stars twinkle above, a distant song,
In the chill of darkness, we all belong.

Frosted breath dances in the air,
Fireplace crackles, warmth to share.
Shadows play on walls so bare,
In these cold nights, love's always there.

Bright Dreams

In the quiet, visions bloom,
Colors swirling, dispelling gloom.
Whispers of hope, they guide the way,
Through the nights that lead to day.

Cotton clouds, a gentle flight,
Carried high, chasing light.
In the stillness, hearts take wing,
Bright dreams come alive, we sing.

Precious Resilience

In stormy seas, we rise anew,
With courage deep, we push on through.
Roots run strong in trembling ground,
A testament to strength we've found.

Through trials faced, we learn to stand,
In every tear, a guiding hand.
Fashioned by fire, we're forged in strife,
Our precious resilience defines our life.

Fables of Frost

On silver branches, tales unfold,
Of whispered dreams and nights so cold.
Fables woven in icy lace,
Memories linger, time can't erase.

Echoes of laughter in the chill,
Frosted mirrors, a magic thrill.
In winter's grasp, stories are born,
Gathering strength for the coming morn.

The Art of Stillness

In quiet moments, peace takes flight,
Glistening silence, a pure delight.
Breath of nature, soft and slow,
Where time stands still and worries go.

Amidst the chaos, find your grace,
In the stillness, a sacred space.
Hearts align with the gentle tide,
The art of stillness, our honest guide.

Nature's Quiet Rebirth

In dawn's soft glow, the earth awakes,
New life emerges, a gentle shake.
Flowers bloom, colors bright,
Nature sings in pure delight.

Birds flit by in cheerful tune,
Sunshine dances, warming June.
Streams flow clear, a sparkling sight,
The world bursts forth in purest light.

Leaves unfurl to greet the sun,
A fresh beginning, all as one.
Joyful hearts come out to play,
In nature's arms, we shall stay.

Melting Hopes

Winter's grip begins to fade,
Beneath the frost, new plans are laid.
Each droplet falls, a silent prayer,
Awakening dreams that linger there.

The sun breaks through, a warming touch,
Life reclaims what it loves much.
In the thaw, pure hopes arise,
As springtime whispers through the skies.

Ice cascades in bright sunlight,
Old shadows flee, new futures ignite.
Nature rejoices in every stream,
Together we rise, united in dream.

Whispers of the Frosted Bough

Silent whispers through the trees,
Frosted branches sway in ease.
Softly falling flakes of white,
Covering all in gentle light.

Each breath a cloud, each step a sigh,
Underneath the vast, grey sky.
Nature sleeps but dreams of spring,
As the world waits for joy to bring.

In the hush of winter's call,
Hope is etched in snowflakes' fall.
Listen closely, hear the sound,
Life will flourish all around.

Beneath the Icy Veil

Beneath the ice, a heart beats slow,
Hidden life that we can't know.
In stillness lies a spark of grace,
Awaiting time to find its place.

The moonlight casts a silver sheen,
On the surface, cold and keen.
Yet deep below, a warmth resides,
Where the pulse of spring abides.

Let patience flow like gentle streams,
For every winter shrouds our dreams.
Under layers, life will strive,
In the dark, we feel alive.

Beneath Frost

Silent whispers in the night,
Nature wrapped in silver light.
A blanket soft, the world asleep,
Beneath the frost, dreams gently creep.

Stars above like diamonds gleam,
In winter's grasp, life seems a dream.
Each breath a cloud, a moment's trace,
Time stands still in this chilly space.

Nature's beauty carved in ice,
A fleeting touch, a silent price.
Echoes of warmth still dance within,
Beneath the frost, new tales begin.

Life's Secrets

Whispers of the trees at dawn,
Carried by the breeze so drawn.
Secrets hidden in the earth,
Awaiting love, awaiting birth.

In shadows deep, we seek the light,
Journey forth through day and night.
Each step a lesson, each tear a seed,
Life's secrets bloom, we take the lead.

The stars above, guides for the soul,
In every struggle, we find our role.
With every heartbeat, stories weave,
In life's grand tapestry, we believe.

Petals in a Snowy Tapestry

Amid the white, petals emerge,
Colors bright, the heart's urge.
A snowy quilt fills the ground,
Softly, beauty can be found.

Frosted blooms in winter's chill,
Silent wonders that time will fill.
In chilly air, their fragrance sways,
Nature's dance on coldest days.

Crystals form on vibrant hues,
Melting hearts with tender views.
Petals whisper, dreams take flight,
In a snowy tapestry, pure delight.

Fragments of Light in Dark Hours

Shadows loom, a sighing night,
Searching for the fragments of light.
Every flicker, a star's embrace,
Guiding souls through this vast space.

Moments lost in time's thick mist,
Yet hope remains, its gentle twist.
In every corner, darkness stays,
Still we find the brighter ways.

Voices echo in tender dreams,
Carried softly on moonlit beams.
Fragments gathered, a radiant spark,
Illuminating paths through the dark.

Blossoms in a Frozen Dream

In winter's clasp, the blossoms freeze,
Petals caught in a chilling breeze.
Yet beneath the surface, warmth resides,
A vibrant world where hope abides.

Dreams of spring in silent hearts,
Waiting patiently as nature imparts.
With every snowflake, stories blend,
In a frozen dream, beginnings mend.

Time will turn, the thaw will come,
Life will burst forth, a vibrant drum.
From frozen ground, new wonders rise,
Blossoms bloom under brighter skies.

Frosted Petals

Petals crisp in morning light,
Glittering like shards of ice.
Nature dons her frosty white,
Whispers of a chill entice.

Silent trees wear silver gowns,
Branches bowed with purest snow.
Beauty in these wintry crowns,
Echoes from the earth below.

Quiet dreams of springtime blooms,
Rest beneath the icy breath.
In the stillness, nature looms,
Life prepares beyond this death.

Each flake falls a soft caress,
Kisses on the sleeping ground.
In their dance, there's tenderness,
Magic in the stillness found.

Yet beneath the layers wide,
Seeds of hope hold their own fate.
In the frost, they still abide,
Waiting for the sun's embrace.

Snow-Covered Blossoms

Blossoms wrapped in winter's white,
Glistening like treasures rare.
Every petal, pure delight,
Cloaked in soft, enchanted air.

Branches bow beneath the load,
Nature's blanket, soft and deep.
Silent whispers, secrets flowed,
In this world, the stillness keeps.

Sunlight peeks through icy veils,
Casting shadows, soft and bright.
Hushed as winter's magic sails,
Over fields in purest light.

Buds awake from frosty dreams,
Yearning for the warmth of spring.
In the silence, nature schemes,
Colors soon will start to sing.

Snowflakes dance on gentle breeze,
Painting landscapes, rich and wide.
In the quiet, heart finds ease,
Waiting for the shift of tide.

The Silent Garden

In the garden, shadows creep,
Where the flowers rest in peace.
Frosty spirits gently weep,
Waiting for a warm release.

Petals frozen in delight,
Colors trapped in nature's hand.
Silent beauty, purest sight,
Dreams of life still understand.

Whispers echo through the trees,
Snowflakes dance on whispered air.
Every branch a memory,
Holding secrets, rich and rare.

In the stillness, time stands still,
Moments caught in silver glow.
Winter's breath, a peaceful thrill,
Binding all in quiet flow.

Yet with time, the thaw will come,
Nature's cycle, life reborn.
In this silence, beats a drum,
A heartbeat, fresh and new morn.

Frost's Embrace

Frost's embrace, a gentle touch,
Whispers secrets in the night.
Nature's breath, so calm and hush,
In the moon's soft, tender light.

Every flake a fleeting kiss,
Carpet wraps the earth with care.
In this world, a moment's bliss,
Frosty dreams in winter's air.

Silent echoes of the past,
Buried deep beneath the chill.
In the stillness, shadows cast,
Memories, they linger still.

Buds of spring hold on with might,
Tucked beneath the frosty seams.
When the golden sun shines bright,
Hope will flourish, bloom in dreams.

So let winter weave its tale,
In the garden, life awaits.
With the thaw, all will unveil,
Beauty bursts through nature's gates.

The Hidden Symphony of Ice

In the stillness of the night,
Crystals whisper secrets bright.
Nature's magic, soft and clear,
Plays a song for all to hear.

Frozen streams and gentle sighs,
Between the branches, beauty lies.
Each flake dances, wild and free,
Uniting earth and sky's decree.

Silvery echoes, calm and shy,
Winter's breath does softly sigh.
Softly glimmers, faint and high,
A symphony beneath the sky.

A hush falls over the land,
Ice and snow, a gentle hand.
Serenading the world in white,
Bringing dreams into the night.

In this realm where stillness reigns,
The heart invites all to remain.
Tuned to echoes that entice,
In the beauty of hidden ice.

Frost Kisses on Flowered Lips

Morning dew with a frosty kiss,
Nature whispers a subtle bliss.
Petals shimmer, soft and bright,
Wrapped in winter's pure delight.

Each bloom's stance, a bold embrace,
Frosted edges, a tender trace.
In this moment, time stands still,
Nature's love is pure and will.

Colors vibrant, kissed by chill,
Life preserved on snowy hill.
Fragrant whispers fill the air,
With every breath, the world is rare.

Underneath the icy veil,
Each flower tells a frosted tale.
Beauty wrapped in winter's arms,
Cradled softly, lost in charms.

A dance of warmth and cold collide,
Where the heart and nature bide.
Frost and petals, a fleeting blend,
This season's grace shall never end.

Beneath Blanket of White

Quiet slumbers, nature sleeps,
Underneath where silence creeps.
A canvas pure, a world anew,
Blanketed in softest hue.

Footprints vanish, time erased,
Memories in white encased.
Each flake falls, a gentle sigh,
Whispers of the earth's lullaby.

Tucked away 'neath winter's shroud,
Every branch stands straight and proud.
The world slows down in purest peace,
Under this soft quilt, worries cease.

Stars above, a sparkling light,
Guide the dreams throughout the night.
The hush surrounds, the heart feels right,
A stillness made of soft delight.

Wonders hide in frosty gleam,
Where reality meets dream.
In the silence, hope ignites,
Beneath the blanket of pure whites.

Crystalline Wishes of Flora

In the garden, softly laid,
Frosty wishes gently played.
Petals shimmer with icy grace,
In nature's pure, enchanting space.

Glistening under moonlit skies,
Flora twinkles, gets lost in sighs.
Crystalline, the beauty grows,
In harmony, the spirit glows.

Each wish cast on the morning dew,
A promise in the sparkling view.
With every frost, a story spun,
In nature's heart, we're all as one.

From the roots to the skies above,
Whispers speak of endless love.
Flora dances, breathes in light,
In crystalline dreams of night.

Wishing stars with petals gleam,
Crafting softly every dream.
In the frost, our hopes combine,
Within the crystal, love will shine.

The Halos of Winter Flora

Underneath the frosted pines,
Whispers weave in silver lines.
Nature cloaked in crystal sheen,
Silent tales of what has been.

Branches bowed with icy grace,
Hidden gems in nature's face.
Winter's touch, so soft yet bold,
Secrets in the air unfold.

Bright halos crown the sleeping earth,
Reminders of each quiet birth.
A dance of light on snowflakes spun,
In the hush, the world's begun.

Voices lost in wintry dreams,
Glittering under sunlit beams.
Every flake, a story penned,
In silence, nature's quiet friend.

As seasons turn, they softly sway,
Winter's bloom, a fleeting stay.
With each breath, the magic swirls,
Halos whispered, nature twirls.

The Unseen Bloom

In shadows deep where colors hide,
A flower breathes, though not in stride.
Silent petals yearn for light,
Wrapped in dreams, away from sight.

With every tear from skies above,
The unseen bloom, it longs for love.
Roots entwined in memories dear,
Whispers linger, close and near.

Softly swaying, a mystery,
In the mind, a blurred history.
The fragrance clings to passing days,
An echo of forgotten ways.

Amidst the chaos, beauty thrives,
Through hidden paths, the heart derives.
Petals bold, yet shyly pressed,
In unseen realms, they find their rest.

A bloom may fade without a sound,
In silence, strength can be profound.
For what is lost may still remain,
The unseen bloom, a soft refrain.

A Chill Beneath the Blossoms

Beneath the blooms, a chill does creep,
Secrets buried, soft and deep.
Petaled whispers hide the frost,
In beauty's breath, the warmth is lost.

Colors vibrant, but spirits shiver,
In their dance, the shadows quiver.
A fleeting spring, the heart must chase,
Time's embrace, a fleeting space.

Each blossom bears the weight of dreams,
Yet all is not as bright as seems.
A hidden frost within their core,
Gentle hints of what's in store.

Around the roots, the chill takes hold,
Stories waiting to be told.
In blossoms' shade, a tender sigh,
Life and death, they intertwine.

As petals fall, the breeze will carry,
The chill beneath, softly wary.
Yet every bloom that flowers bright,
Holds the chill with pure delight.

A Blooming Mystery

In twilight's hush, a secret stirs,
A blooming mystery, nature's whirs.
Bud unfolds with whispered grace,
Surprises live in every space.

Colors merge in soft embrace,
A quiet thrill, a hidden trace.
The heart of petals, tightly curled,
Reveals the magic of the world.

Mornings break with fragrant hints,
Unveiling forms as light begins.
Each blossom tells of tales untold,
In every hue, a story bold.

A kaleidoscope of dreams and fears,
Rippling through the passing years.
Nature's riddle, always near,
In every bloom, the truth sincere.

As twilight falls, the mystery fades,
Yet in the heart, the magic stays.
For life's a cycle, blooms renew,
A mystery shared in every hue.

Parables of Growth in Frozen Times

In winter's grasp, the seeds lie still,
Dreams wrapped in snow, untouched by chill.
Beneath the frost, their whispers sway,
Yearning for warmth, to greet the day.

As sunlight breaks the frozen night,
New life awakens, soft and bright.
Each tiny bud a tale untold,
Of strength in silence, brave and bold.

Roots dig deep, anchored in trust,
From frozen earth, they rise, robust.
Patience, the key, as seasons turn,
In stillness forged, the spirits burn.

With every thaw, the stories flow,
Of battles faced in chill and snow.
From icy dreams to vibrant hues,
The journey's path, we must peruse.

In frozen times when hope seems shy,
Growth stirs softly, reaching high.
In nature's clock, we learn to see,
The parables of growth set free.

The Quiet Flicker of Flora's Heart

In shadows soft where petals hide,
A flicker glows, where dreams reside.
Flora's heart beats slow and sheer,
In the hush, its whispers clear.

Beneath the leaves, the secrets sleep,
In silent cradles, deep and deep.
Each pulse a promise, brave and mild,
Nature's breath, serene, instilled.

When twilight falls, the world slips by,
Yet in the dark, the colors fly.
A quiet dance, the blooms embrace,
In every shadow, love finds space.

The earth, a canvas, bold and vast,
In every flicker, shadows cast.
Flora's heart, a gentle spark,
Illuminates the tranquil dark.

In softest tones, the whispers rise,
A quiet flicker, in twilight skies.
As nature breathes, hearts intertwine,
In peace, the flicker shall define.

Radiant Secrets in the Glacial Light

In realms of ice, where stories freeze,
Secrets twinkle, dance with ease.
Beneath the glimmer, buried deep,
Radiant dreams that time shall keep.

Crystals form and patterns weep,
Echoes of life in silence creep.
In the stillness, beauty reigns,
While nature's pulse beats through the veins.

Glistening shards of pure delight,
Reveal the shadows, curtain light.
Whispers carried on a breeze,
Tell tales of joy, of love's sweet tease.

Through frost's embrace, the colors climb,
Each radiant secret speaks of time.
In glacial glow, the world anew,
Awakens dreams that once we knew.

Amid the chill, there's warmth inside,
Radiant secrets, winter's guide.
As daybreak breaks the icy night,
We learn to cherish, hold the light.

Layers of Cold

Beneath the frost, secrets hide,
Silent whispers of the slide.
Each layer, a story untold,
Wrapped in the blanket of cold.

Breath of winter, crisp and clear,
The quiet world, no sign of fear.
Chill wraps around, a tender hold,
Embracing the layers of cold.

Footprints imprinted on the white,
Marking paths in the fading light.
A tapestry woven, bold,
Nature's secrets, gently rolled.

Frozen rivers, still and deep,
In their silence, memories keep.
Time stands still, both young and old,
In the embrace of the cold.

A breath, a pause, nature's sigh,
The world beneath a silver sky.
With every layer, joy unfolds,
Feeling the layers of cold.

Crystalline Blooms Unveiled

Under moonlight, magic glows,
Crystalline blooms, a beauty shows.
Petals of ice, so pure, so bright,
Glistening softly in the night.

Nature's gems upon the ground,
Whispers of beauty all around.
Each bloom tells a tale of grace,
In this frost-kissed, wondrous place.

Gently swaying in the breeze,
These fragile blooms, with such ease.
Sparkling jewels, truths unveiled,
Crystalline treasures, never failed.

In the stillness, dreams take flight,
As crystals dance in the soft light.
Winter's brush, a canvas sailed,
Bringing forth blooms, unassailed.

So let us cherish each fine sight,
In frosty gardens, pure delight.
Where every winter's tale has hailed,
The crystalline blooms unveiled.

Pathways Through Frost

The world ahead cloaked in white,
Pathways twist under silver light.
Every step, a crunching sound,
In this winter wonder, I'm bound.

Trees stand tall, their branches bare,
In the crispness, I breathe the air.
Footsteps mark where I have trod,
In the blanket that winter's flawed.

Shadows dance on the frozen ground,
Mysteries in silence abound.
Nature's artwork, a beauty sought,
In the pathways that frost has wrought.

Wind whispers secrets through the trees,
Carrying tales upon the breeze.
Every turn, a story caught,
In the pathways where frost is sought.

A journey through, a wandering soul,
Guided by nature's gentle scroll.
In every corner, a wonder caught,
Through pathways built by frost, I'm taught.

Whispers of Frosted Petals

Delicate petals, kissed by frost,
In their beauty, I find the cost.
Softly shimmering in the light,
Whispers of winter in their flight.

Nature's breath upon each bloom,
Silent secrets in their room.
Glistening softly, stories told,
Frosted petals, brave and bold.

With every touch, a shiver shakes,
A dance of chill, the world awakes.
In the garden, the truth unfolds,
In whispers of frost, love beholds.

Echoes resonating in the air,
Frost's artistry, a dance so rare.
Every petal, a story of old,
Whispers of frost as they unfold.

The sun will rise, but for now, I stay,
In this world where the frost holds sway.
Wrapped in beauty, my heart beholds,
The whispers of frosted petals, bold.

A Reflection in Ice

Stillness held in frozen grace,
Mirrored skies in chilly space.
Whispers dance on surfaces clear,
Nature's hush, a world sincere.

Moonlight kisses icy streams,
Shadows weave in silver beams.
Each breath clouds, a moment rare,
In this realm, hearts lay bare.

Footsteps crunch on frosty ground,
Echoes linger, softly sound.
A solitary figure waits,
Time suspended, as it creates.

Reflections shimmer, tales unfold,
Stories etched in hues of cold.
Beauty found in still despair,
Frozen realms, a secret share.

To walk this path is to embrace,
Life's soft whispers, a gentle trace.
In every flake, a fleeting song,
A reflection where we belong.

Petals of the North Wind

Beneath the boughs, petals drift light,
Carried softly by the night.
Whispers travel on the breeze,
Nature's tune in rustling leaves.

Petals twirl with story's grace,
Each a dream in time and space.
North winds dance, a lively game,
Bringing life, yet nothing's the same.

Colors blend in twilight's glow,
Gentle fragrances bestow.
A journey shared by those who roam,
In petal paths, we find our home.

Silence speaks in dusky shades,
Murals painted, nature's trades.
Softly falling, moments blend,
A tapestry that has no end.

The north wind guides, its tender touch,
Petals fall, they mean so much.
In every touch, a promise made,
Life's fleeting dance in soft cascade.

Serenade of the Frosted Grove

In a grove where silence sings,
Frosted boughs bear nature's wings.
A serenade of crystal hues,
Whispers carried on the dews.

Leaves adorned with icy lace,
Frozen notes in quiet grace.
The wind, a bard with tales untold,
Each breath a story, young and old.

Light cascades through branches bare,
Dancing shadows everywhere.
A symphony of life now sleeps,
In winter's hold, the stillness creeps.

Beneath the snow, seeds lie awake,
Waiting for the thaw, the break.
In frosted dreams, a spark ignites,
Hope is woven in the nights.

Serenade through darkest tide,
Life's sweet promise, a gentle guide.
Frosted grove, a sacred space,
Where time stands still in nature's grace.

The Soft Heart of January

January whispers soft and low,
A tender heart beneath the snow.
Promises wrapped in chilly air,
A hopeful pause, a moment rare.

As dawn breaks bright, the world awakes,
In frosted light, a new path makes.
Traces of warmth in every chill,
A canvas where winter's dreams fulfill.

Silver threads of frost entwine,
In each breath, a soft divine.
Hopes emerge with each sunrise,
In January's embrace, we rise.

With every step, the pulse of earth,
Whispers secrets of rebirth.
The soft heart beats, a tender call,
In the stillness, we find it all.

January holds the promise clear,
Of dreams to come in every year.
In its gentle arms, we find our way,
Guided by the light of day.

Echoes of an Icy Dawn

Silent whispers kiss the ground,
Morning light begins to sound.
Shadows dance on glistening frost,
In this world, winter's embossed.

Breath of dawn in chilling air,
Nature wakes without a care.
Gentle hues of pink and blue,
Promise of a day anew.

Crystalline trees bow low with grace,
A fragile beauty, time can trace.
Echoes of the night's soft sigh,
As the sun climbs, shadows fly.

Frosty patterns, delicate lace,
Art of winter's cold embrace.
Each moment, fleeting and bright,
In frozen realms of pure delight.

So, we stand in awe and peace,
As the icy whispers cease.
Echoes fade in morning's glow,
Winter's magic, pure and slow.

In the Shade of Frost

Beneath the branches, silence reigns,
Nature's beauty, no chains.
In the shade where frost does play,
Memories of a colder day.

Glimmers sparkling on the ground,
Frozen gems that once were found.
Brittle leaves in silence rest,
Amongst the icy, wintry vest.

Softly calls the winter bird,
In the stillness, not a word.
All around, a hush profound,
In the shade, a whispering sound.

Time stands still in frosty air,
Beauty held with gentle care.
Every breath, a cloud of white,
In the coolness of twilight.

Winter's grace in softest form,
In this moment, still and warm.
Embrace the shade, the frosty air,
In the stillness, peace laid bare.

Resplendent Under Ice

Beneath the crystalline expanse,
Nature sings a frozen dance.
Colors vibrant, yet so cold,
In ice's grip, beauty unfolds.

Sparkling rivers, flow of glass,
Moments fleeting, never last.
Each reflection, prism bright,
Glimmers softly in the light.

Tallest mountains dressed in white,
Guardians of the starry night.
Silent echoes fill the space,
Hushed and holy, winter's grace.

Underneath the icy crust,
Life is waiting, as we trust.
Every layer, secret kept,
Silent stories softly slept.

Resplendent under frost and freeze,
Whispers carried on the breeze.
Nature's canvas, bold and clear,
Winter's song for all to hear.

Frozen Whispers

In the stillness, whispers freeze,
Secrets carried on the breeze.
Frosty breath of winter's night,
In the dark, a glimmering light.

Silent shadows glide and sway,
Murmurs of the dying day.
Branches creak under the weight,
Nature's song—a blend of fate.

Fleeting moments, sharp and bright,
Draped in silver, purest light.
Every flake a tale to tell,
Frozen whispers, casting spells.

Snowflakes swirl like dancers grand,
Catching dreams upon the land.
In this world, where silence sings,
Frozen thoughts on crystal wings.

As the night wraps all in peace,
Winter's breath will never cease.
Frozen whispers, soft and low,
In the dark, a soft hello.

Beauty Amidst the Chill

In the quiet of frost's embrace,
Beauty glimmers, soft and rare.
Crystals dance on the frozen lake,
Whispers of winter fill the air.

Beneath the branches, silence reigns,
Snowflakes flutter, twirling down.
Nature's wonder, a hush remains,
A tranquil moment, winter's crown.

Footprints trace where dreams have walked,
In the glow of a pale moon's light.
The world is still, yet softly talks,
Of beauty found in every night.

Time pauses in the frosty breeze,
As shadows stretch on ivory floors.
Each breath a cloud in the cold air,
A secret shared between woods and shores.

With every chill, the heart shall swell,
For beauty lives amidst the frost.
In winter's arms, we weave our spell,
In peace, we find what once was lost.

Dreams in a Winter Landscape

Fields of white stretch far and wide,
A canvas pure, a vision clear.
In the hush, our dreams reside,
Every heartbeat close and near.

Frosted trees, like sentinels,
Guard the secrets held within.
Echoes of laughter, soft spells,
Where joy and silence gleam and spin.

Underneath the velvet sky,
Stars twinkle like distant dreams.
Nature sings a lullaby,
As snowflakes fall in silver streams.

Crisp air fills our lungs with cheer,
Painting whispers across our skin.
In these moments, crystal clear,
We discover where love begins.

In the stillness, we find grace,
Every shadow a tale to tell.
Winter's landscape holds its place,
In dreams where hearts and hope dwell.

Tales of the Icy Petals

In gardens cloaked by winter's breath,
Petals shimmer, frost-kissed, bright.
Each blossom tells a tale of death,
And rebirth in the pale moonlight.

Frozen whispers, secrets shared,
Lifting hearts in the chilly air.
Icy patterns, nature's dared,
Painted on leaves with gentle care.

A soft touch in the starkness found,
Underneath the starry veil.
Life persists, though the world is bound,
In every petal, a timeless tale.

As shadows dance on snowy ground,
Mysteries weave through the trees.
In the silence, beauty's found,
Where petals glisten with winter's breeze.

The stories linger, faint yet clear,
Of moments caught in icy threads.
With every beat, there's warmth, my dear,
In petals draped where hope still spreads.

Softness in the Winter Light

Gentle rays in a world of frost,
Touching earth with a warming grace.
Colors softened, lines are lost,
In winter's light, we find our place.

Whispers travel on the cold breeze,
As sunbeams glint on patches white.
Every heart begins to ease,
Embracing the glow of winter's light.

Through the trees, shadows softly play,
Creating patterns on the ground.
In the quiet of a winter day,
Every silence is a sound.

Forgotten dreams in the pale sun,
Awaken gently from their sleep.
In the warmth, all hearts are one,
In the light, our shadows deep.

Thus we tread beneath the skies,
In warmth that twinkles, fades, and sways.
Finding softness in the lies,
The winter light, our hearts, obeys.

Nature's Soft Slumber

In the hush of twilight's call,
Whispers echo through the hall.
Stars begin their gentle glow,
As the world finds peace below.

Leaves rest on the mossy ground,
Silence wrapping all around.
Dreams of spring in hearts confined,
Softly waiting, intertwined.

Moonlight dances on the stream,
Casting shadows, weaving dream.
Nature breathes a slumber deep,
In her arms, all life will sleep.

Crickets sing a lullaby,
Beneath the vast and starlit sky.
In the dark, a nightbird's tune,
Sings of peace beneath the moon.

Morning breaks with golden light,
Waking nature from the night.
With the dawn, new hopes arise,
In the glow of brightening skies.

Petals Amidst the Chill

Frosted mornings, crisp and clear,
Petals trembling, full of fear.
Nature's beauty shivers low,
In the winds that softly blow.

Colors fade, yet softly cling,
Hope beneath the winter's sting.
Petals brave the icy breath,
Dancing still, defying death.

Underneath the silver veil,
Life persists, it will not pale.
Warmth resides in every hue,
Waiting for the sun to break through.

Each blossom holds a secret bright,
Living in the cold, not fright.
In their hearts, the springtime waits,
For the thaw that rejuvenates.

Where the winter's chill does reign,
Love and beauty still remain.
Petals whisper, 'We are here,
Holding on through every fear.'

Shadows of Frozen Flora

In the garden, shadows creep,
Frozen whispers, secrets keep.
Delicate as dream's own thread,
Life suspended, softly led.

Twilight falls on icy blooms,
Silence deepens, night consumes.
Hollow echoes lull the trees,
As shadows dance upon the breeze.

Frosty fingers trace the ground,
Painting stories all around.
Flowers bow beneath the weight,
Of the stillness, stoic fate.

Yet beneath that frosted guise,
Life's resilience softly lies.
From the cold, they draw their strength,
In the shadows, blooms at length.

With the dawn, a spark ignites,
Beneath the frost, new hope ignites.
From frozen roots, new life will spring,
In the shadows, warmth shall bring.

The Secret Life of Frost

Cloaked in winter's shimmering light,
Frost weaves magic through the night.
Each crystal tells a tale so grand,
Of whispered dreams across the land.

Glistening on the windowpane,
Nature's art, a sweet refrain.
Every flake a story spun,
In the silence of the sun.

Gentle patterns, tracing time,
Nature's verses, soft and prime.
In the chill, a heart beats strong,
Frost revealing where we belong.

Secrets hidden in the air,
Life concealed in winter's stare.
With each breath, a promise flows,
Life anew as the morning glows.

So listen close to frost's soft sighs,
In its touch, the magic lies.
Beyond the chill, the warmth of grace,
In the secret life, we find our place.

Dappled Sunlight on a Brisk Morning

The morning light breaks through the trees,
Casting shadows on the ground with ease.
Leaves flutter softly in the gentle breeze,
Awakening dreams that roam like bees.

Birds chirp sweetly, a melodic call,
Nature's symphony, enchanting all.
Dew on the grass, a sparkling thrall,
A moment of magic, so pure and small.

The world stirs slowly, a dance of light,
Colors painted in a warm delight.
Each step forward, the heart takes flight,
In dappled sunlight, everything feels right.

Clouds drift lazily in the cobalt sky,
Whispering secrets as they float by.
Time slips gently, oh, how it flies,
In the embrace of morning's sighs.

With every breath, new hopes are bright,
Grounded in peace, yet yearning for height.
A brisk morning beckons, pure and light,
In dappled sunlight, the soul takes flight.

The Art of Soft Resilience

In the shadows, stillness finds a way,
Gentle whispers guide the heart to stay.
Through trials faced, we learn to sway,
Embracing storms that come our way.

Soft resilience blooms beneath the ground,
In quiet strength, true hope is found.
Like tender blossoms, all around,
We rise again, with love unbound.

Each scar and wound becomes a part,
Tracing the map of a courageous heart.
In the silence, we find our art,
A tapestry woven, set apart.

With every challenge, we learn to bend,
Transforming pain into a friend.
Through darkest nights, our spirits mend,
In soft resilience, we transcend.

The journey flows like a river's song,
A testament that we all belong.
In unity, where we grow strong,
The art of softness carries us along.

Echoes of Life in the Chill

In the stillness of a winter's day,
Echoes linger, then drift away.
Life murmurs softly beneath the gray,
A whispered promise of spring's ballet.

Frosted branches, shimmering white,
Capture moments in fleeting light.
Every breath forms a cloud, a sight,
Echoes of life, a soft invite.

Silence blankets the world in peace,
While in the heart, warm dreams increase.
Nature pauses, calls for release,
In winter's chill, we find our fleece.

The crackling fire, a warm embrace,
Reflects the glow upon each face.
Memories dance in this quiet space,
Echoes of life, a sacred trace.

Time slows down, the world feels still,
In the icy breath, a gentle thrill.
Each moment cherished, a heartfelt fill,
Echoes of life in the chill.

Snow's Embrace on Tender Leaves

In winter's fold, the world is hushed,
Snowflakes fall, the air is brushed.
Softly kissing the tender leaves,
Nature cradles as it weaves.

Blankets of white, a tender care,
Covering greens in a loving layer.
Each flake rests light, a quiet prayer,
Whispers of peace linger in the air.

Branches bow low with snowy weight,
Holding secrets of the quiet state.
Whirls of wonder in nature's crate,
Snow's embrace ensures our fate.

As slowly drifts the winter chill,
Every leaf's heart beats still.
In this moment, time stands still,
Snow's embrace fulfills the thrill.

Life holds tight, despite the frost,
In each soft flake, beauty embossed.
Tender leaves know, though they're lost,
Snow's embrace comes at a cost.

Blossoms of Bittersweet

In gardens where the shadows play,
The blooms unfold their hues of gray.
Each petal whispers tales of woe,
Yet fragrance lingers, soft and slow.

A dusk that paints the skies in fire,
Reminds us all of lost desire.
With every sigh, the memories creep,
In bittersweet moments, we still reap.

Amidst the joy, the heart will ache,
For love's embrace, it cannot shake.
But in the twilight's gentle falling,
The bittersweet blooms keep us calling.

Through seasons change, the roots grow deep,
In soil where old secrets sleep.
The blossoms shade our heavy hearts,
Yet in their colors, hope imparts.

So let the bittersweet remind,
Of tangled tales in love we bind.
With every bloom, a fleeting chance,
To dance again in memory's trance.

Frosty Reverie

Beneath the chill of winter's breath,
The world lies silent, wrapped in death.
A silver hush drapes every tree,
As whispered dreams float wild and free.

In frosty realms where shadows dance,
The moonlight's glow ignites a trance.
Each breath a cloud, a world anew,
As hopes arise in morning's dew.

The air is crisp, each note a sound,
Of nature's heart where peace is found.
In every flake that drifts and sways,
A symphony of winter's praise.

Amidst the stillness, life will thrive,
In frosty lands where hearts revive.
Each sparkling crystal, pure and bright,
Reflects the beauty of the night.

So let the snowflakes softly fall,
And cover earth with nature's call.
In frosty reveries we find,
The grace of winter, beautifully blind.

Silence of the Snow Filled Fields

In fields that stretch 'neath frozen skies,
Silence reigns where beauty lies.
The snowflakes blanket every hue,
Transforming lands to purest white view.

Each step is muffled, soft and slow,
In winter's grasp, the breezes blow.
The whispers of the earth held tight,
In snow-filled fields, a tranquil sight.

The quiet holds a sacred song,
As nature hums its gentle throng.
In every drift, the secrets keep,
The silence wraps the world in sleep.

With every sunrise, shadows fade,
Yet still the heart feels winter's blade.
In frozen breaths, we find our way,
Through snow-filled fields where dreams can stay.

So wander forth through winter's tale,
Embrace the silence, never pale.
For in the stillness, depth does unfold,
A world of wonders waiting, untold.

Beneath the Glimmering Ice

Beneath the calm of glimmering ice,
The waters hide a world so nice.
With light that dances, shadows play,
In secret realms where dreams can sway.

Each crystal formed, a story told,
Of silent depths, of treasures bold.
The whispers echo, soft and clear,
In icy depths where souls draw near.

The frozen lakes hold ancient dreams,
In twilight's glow, where starlight beams.
Beneath the surface, life persists,
In every ripple, silence kissed.

So let us tread with gentle grace,
Upon the ice, a fragile space.
In glimmer's glow, we find our peace,
And watch the magic never cease.

For in the winter's cold embrace,
We find our way to nature's place.
Beneath the glimmering ice we stand,
In awe of life's enchanted land.

Graceful Acts in a Frigid Frame

In winter's chill, the world does pause,
Soft whispers drift, without a cause.
A glance of warmth, a gentle embrace,
Graceful acts in this frozen space.

The snowflakes fall like silent sighs,
Covering dreams beneath gray skies.
Yet hearts ignite with glowing sparks,
In every breath, love leaves its marks.

Through icy paths, true warmth shall grow,
In shared moments, light will flow.
With kindness wrapped in tender seams,
We weave our tapestry of dreams.

As branches bare reach for the sun,
Together we stand, two become one.
For in this frame, so frigid, stark,
Our spirits soar, igniting the dark.

In the quiet hush of winter's breath,
We find our strength, we dance with death.
With each soft step, the world ignites,
Graceful acts, our shared delights.

The Daring Dance of Undying Spirit

In shadows deep where fears reside,
The spirit rises, fierce with pride.
With every falter, every fall,
The daring dance ignites us all.

Through storms that howl and winds that roar,
We face the night, and seek for more.
With burning hearts and steadfast eyes,
We reach for dreams that fill the skies.

The rhythm pulses, vibrant, alive,
In this grand struggle, we will thrive.
Each challenge met, each wound we bear,
A testament to hope laid bare.

We spin and twirl, unbroken, free,
In every step, our legacy.
We chase the dawn, defy the night,
A daring dance, our spirits bright.

For in our hearts, the fire glows,
A fierce resolve that only grows.
With every beat, we claim our part,
The undying spirit — a work of art.

Petals in the Pale Light

In morning's hush, the petals fall,
Soft whispers of nature's call.
Beneath the dawn's pale, golden hue,
Life awakens, fresh and new.

Each blossom holds a secret rare,
A fragrant story in the air.
They dance with grace in softest breeze,
In tender moments, hearts find ease.

Through sunlight's kiss and shadows cast,
A fleeting beauty, meant to last.
In every hue, the world delights,
Petals shining in pale light.

With gentle hands, we gather close,
These lovely gifts, a cherished prose.
In every petal, joy unfolds,
A tapestry of warmth enfolds.

Underneath the vast, open sky,
We watch the petals drift and fly.
A symphony in vibrant display,
Petals dancing with hope today.

Visions of Color Against a White Canvas

Upon the canvas, pure and bright,
Dreams emerge in bursts of light.
Each stroke a tale, each hue a song,
Visions of color, a world so strong.

With reds that blaze and blues that sing,
The heart finds voice in everything.
Greens of nature, warm and bold,
The stories of life, vividly told.

In chaos splashed, we find our peace,
With every shade, our fears release.
A tapestry of thoughts entwined,
Unfolding views, the heart aligned.

Against the white, the colors dance,
A vibrant hum, a wondrous chance.
From darkness springs the light anew,
Visions painted, deep and true.

In every corner, creation glows,
These strokes of wonder, love bestows.
With hearts ignited, souls set free,
Visions of color, our symphony.

The Dance of Frosted Petals

In the morning light they gleam,
Petals frail, a fragile dream.
Whispers soft, the breeze will send,
Nature's waltz, without an end.

Beneath the trees, they sway and play,
Colors brightened by the day.
Each one tells a story sweet,
In the sun's warm, golden seat.

Frosted edges, they twinkle bright,
Dancing joyfully in the light.
With each turn, they find their grace,
A lovely, fluid, soft embrace.

When evening falls, they gently close,
Carried home by evening's prose.
In slumber deep, the petals rest,
Dreaming of a world, blessed.

Tomorrow brings another show,
As soft winds whisper to and fro.
The dance resumes, a timeless thread,
In nature's quilt, where dreams are bred.

Lullabies of the Cold

Whispers wrapped in winter's hush,
A melody that makes us blush.
Stars twinkle in the frosty skies,
As snowflakes fall, and silence sighs.

Chill winds sing through the empty trees,
A symphony of winter's ease.
Blankets soft, all layered white,
Lullabies fading into night.

Moonlight drapes the world in peace,
A tranquil spell, a sweet release.
The cold embraces all it meets,
In this stillness, our heartbeats.

The gentle crunch beneath our feet,
Echoes soft, a rhythmic beat.
Nature breathes in cool repose,
As winter's song begins to pose.

Let the world be slow and calm,
In this chilly, soothing balm.
Lullabies echo, we won't fear,
In frosty arms, we hold what's near.

A Garden Wrapped in Lace

Delicate blooms in winter's clasp,
Each petal hints at spring's soft grasp.
A lace of frost on every leaf,
Nature's artwork, pure belief.

Colors muted, resting low,
In this quiet, soft tableau.
With morning dew, they gleam and glow,
A frozen dream, a gentle show.

Footsteps crunch on paths well-tread,
Through the garden where dreams are spread.
Every breath of air sings clear,
As time pauses, holding dear.

With whispers shared amongst the twirl,
Petals dance, in delicate swirl.
Frosted lace that graces them all,
A garden waiting for the call.

Awake, dear blooms, when spring arrives,
To paint the world where beauty thrives.
For every season we will trace,
The love entwined in this sweet space.

When Snowflakes Sing

Dancing down from skies so grey,
Snowflakes twirl in grand ballet.
Each one unique, a fleeting song,
Carried sweetly, all day long.

On rooftops high, they gently land,
Creating blankets, soft and grand.
Whispers rise as children play,
In the wonder of winter's sway.

With every flake, a note is played,
In the silence, joy displayed.
A world transformed, pure and bright,
When snowflakes sing, all hearts take flight.

The laughter echoes, spirits soar,
As winter's magic opens doors.
In the glow of sunset's hue,
The snowflakes sing, a tune so true.

So let us dance in winter's arms,
Embrace the chill, the season's charms.
For when snowflakes sing, we find,
A gentle rhythm, softly kind.

Unfurling in the Cold

In the hush of winter's breath,
Petals curl beneath the frost,
Cautious buds await the thaw,
In silence, life pays no cost.

They stretch towards a muted sun,
Unfurling with a gentle grace,
Wrapped in whispers, soft and slow,
In the cold, they find their place.

Frozen ground is not the end,
But a pause in nature's song,
With every drop of melting ice,
A promise that won't be long.

Hope awakens among the shards,
As crystal blankets melt away,
New beginnings breathe and sigh,
In the heart of winter's day.

From the stillness, life will rise,
Unfurling in the cold embrace,
Each bud a tale of resilience,
Of finding warmth in every space.

Life's Quiet Defiance

In shadows cast by doubt and fear,
A bloom persists, though small and meek,
With every glance that passes by,
It stands alone, defying bleak.

Whispers stir in gentle winds,
As leaves unfurl with vibrant hue,
Silent voices call for change,
Life's quiet strength shines ever true.

Through storm and strife, it finds a way,
Roots delving deep in stubborn ground,
Each tendril fights against the weight,
A testament where hope is found.

Though winds may howl, and skies may cry,
This spirit dances through the rain,
With every droplet, it will thrive,
In life's defiance, there's no pain.

So let the world around it roar,
For in the heart, it holds its ground,
Life's quiet defiance shall endure,
And flourish where love can be found.

Threads of Green in a Silver World

Amidst the frost, the earth lies bare,
Yet whispers rise in hidden stems,
From icy roots, life finds its voice,
Threads of green, nature's diadems.

Beneath the silver, shadows mingle,
Emerald dreams wait to awaken,
Snowflakes dance with softest grace,
In every heart, a promise shaken.

As crystals glimmer in the light,
Buds prepare for their grand debut,
Each strand a pulse of luscious hope,
In a world wrapped in chilling blue.

The sun returns with gentle touch,
Kisses lost in frost's embrace,
And through the song of melting ice,
Green threads weave a warming lace.

So let us watch as life unfolds,
In hues of jade against the grey,
Threads of green in a silver world,
A tapestry that leads the way.

Frosty Lullabies of the Earth

In the stillness of the night,
Whispers weave through breath of snow,
Frosty lullabies softly sung,
A gentle blanket, peace to show.

Moonlit strokes on frozen fields,
Crystals twinkle, stars come down,
Nature's heart, in slumber deep,
A quiet hush, a silvery crown.

Beneath the frost, a rhythm beats,
As life rests in its crystal shell,
Each flake a note in winter's song,
A melody that's cast a spell.

Muffled dreams of spring arise,
In every whispered, frosty breath,
The earth cradles hopes anew,
In lullabies that dance with death.

So let us linger in the chill,
Embrace the beauty in the cold,
For even in the frost's embrace,
Lies the warmth of stories told.

Silent Echos of Blooming Hopes

In the quiet of dawn's embrace,
Whispers of dreams begin to rise.
Petals unfurl, a gentle grace,
Underneath the vast, blue skies.

Moments linger, soft and clear,
Echoes of laughter fill the air.
With every heartbeat, hope draws near,
Life blooms boldly, without a care.

In shadows lost, yet shining bright,
Silent hopes weave through the seams.
Amidst the dark, they find the light,
Guided by the realm of dreams.

A garden born from tender seeds,
Courage breaking through the ground.
In every heart, a seed still pleads,
For love and hope to be profound.

So rise with grace, embrace the flow,
Let every petal dance and sway.
In silent echoes, hearts will grow,
And find their way to brighter day.

Sparkling Dewdrops in a Shimmering Chill

Morning breaks with glistening grace,
Dewdrops sparkle on the grass.
In the quiet, a fleeting trace,
Nature's jewels, moments pass.

Each droplet holds a world so pure,
Reflecting light in shimmering hues.
In the stillness, hearts endure,
As the chilly breeze imbues.

Frosty breaths paint the landscape white,
Whispering secrets to the trees.
Life unfolds in the pale light,
Carried softly on the breeze.

Beneath the cold, warmth dares to dream,
Roots reach deep into the earth.
In every twinkling-like sunbeam,
Hopes arise, awaiting rebirth.

In the silence of the morning chill,
Nature's charm captivates the heart.
Dewdrops gleam and souls stand still,
Crafting beauty in the art.

Dreams Sketched in Frost

Underneath the winter's breath,
Dreams are painted on the glass.
Intricate patterns of life and death,
Whispers of time in a fleeting pass.

Frosted edges, delicate lines,
Each one tells a hidden tale.
In the stillness, magic shines,
In every breath, a wistful veil.

Winter nights cradle each desire,
In the shadows, dreams ignite.
With every flake, a heart's fire,
Sketching futures, pure and bright.

Nature holds a canvas vast,
Colors merge in a soft embrace.
The fleeting moments cannot last,
Yet beauty lingers, leaves a trace.

In the frost, we find our way,
Navigating paths we seek.
Dreams etched in ice, come what may,
Resilience strong, though spirits weak.

Nature's Resilience Against the Cold

Beneath the frost, life finds its song,
Roots entwined in the earth below.
In the harshness, it grows strong,
Resilient hearts, a steady flow.

Each winter's chill, a test of will,
But nature fortifies in time.
Through frozen nights, the spirits thrill,
Seeking light, taking each climb.

In every branch, a story weaves,
Against the cold, they reach for sun.
Life perseveres, and hope believes,
A journey shared by everyone.

Amidst the snow, colors emerge,
Wildflowers bloom with radiant grace.
In resilience, their hearts converge,
Nature's art in every place.

Beneath white blankets, seeds await,
A promise kept through the darkest nights.
With every dawn, they celebrate,
The warmth of spring, softening sights.

The Color of Silence

In whispers soft, shadows creep,
Colors blend where secrets sleep.
The world holds breath, the night unfolds,
A canvas vast, where silence molds.

Stars like whispers, calm and bright,
Paint the dark with gentle light.
Each moment still, each heartbeat slow,
In silence, all the wonders grow.

Echoes linger in the air,
Invisible threads, a gentle snare.
Nature sighs with quiet grace,
Infinite calm in this sacred space.

Time stands still, as though to pause,
In this realm, no need for laws.
The hush envelops, a tender balm,
In the quiet, we find our calm.

Colors dance in muted tones,
In the silence, beauty roams.
A world unseen, yet deeply felt,
In the hush, our hearts can melt.

Forgotten Growth

Beneath the soil, roots entwine,
Whispers of life in the dark, divine.
Hidden stories, dreams take flight,
In silent gardens, out of sight.

Moss-covered stones and fallen leaves,
Tell of time that gently weaves.
Fragile sprouts break through the past,
In the stillness, shadows cast.

Memories linger in soft decay,
Where sunlight fades at close of day.
New beginnings in old remains,
Life's resilience, truth sustains.

The forest breathes, a sacred space,
In every crack, a warm embrace.
Forgotten seeds, the earth's deep sigh,
In their silence, hopes can fly.

Within the cracks of ancient wood,
Nature's whispers, understood.
In lost corners, potential found,
In the stillness, growth unbound.

An Unfurling in Stillness

Petals fold like secrets deep,
In morning light, their silence keep.
Each bloom awakens slowly, still,
Unfurling dreams with gentle will.

Quiet moments hold the dawn,
As fragile colors stretch and yawn.
A sigh of life in the cool air,
In stillness, beauty lays bare.

Nature breathes, a soft refrain,
In every whisper, joy and pain.
The world spins slow, yet time will race,
In silent growth, we find our place.

Each leaf a story, soft and bright,
Caught in rays of tender light.
An unfurling, a heart's release,
In stillness found, our sweet increase.

Within the hush, the magic flows,
Unseen wonders, soft as snow.
In slowest moments, life will bloom,
In trance of stillness, joys consume.

Ether of the Cold

In the ether where frost resides,
Whispers wander, and stillness hides.
Chill descends on the silent night,
A world wrapped softly, dimmed in white.

Breath of winter, crisp and clear,
Silent echoes, cold yet near.
Each flake dances, soft and free,
In the ether, pure tranquility.

The moon casts shadows, silvered dreams,
Through frosted trees, the quiet beams.
A calm descends, the heart's embrace,
In the cold, a sacred space.

Every shiver, a tender sigh,
Nature's lullaby, soft and shy.
In bitter winds, the warmth is sought,
In the stillness, peace is wrought.

Ether swirls, both rich and pale,
A tapestry woven, a soft veil.
In the cold, we find the glow,
Of fleeting moments, yet to know.

Awakening beneath Layers of Ice

Silent whispers through the frost,
Nature holds her breath and waits.
Underneath the frozen crust,
Life stirs softly, shaping fates.

Crystals glisten in the light,
Reflecting rays of warming sun.
Each shard glows with ancient might,
A promise that spring's not done.

In the stillness, dreams take flight,
Hidden realms begin to wake.
Hope emerges from the night,
With every crack, the earth will shake.

Beneath the ice, a world anew,
Hidden seeds begin to swell.
Awakening in shades of blue,
This secret story, ours to tell.

Wait we must for the final thaw,
As thawing hearts reclaim their part.
In the quiet, nature's law,
Awakens in each beating heart.

The Beauty of Quietude

In the stillness, time stands still,
Snowflakes dance on gentle breeze.
Nature whispers, calm and chill,
Wrapped in peace, the world at ease.

Softly blanketed in white,
Every sound seems far away.
In the hush, a tranquil sight,
Winter's grace in pure display.

Frosted trees, a silver crown,
Branches bow beneath the weight.
In this silence, there's no frown,
Only beauty to create.

Moments pass like fleeting dreams,
Captured in the quiet air.
Every glimmer, light that beams,
Tells a tale of magic rare.

So let us dwell in this embrace,
Where chaos fades and thoughts align.
In stillness, we find our place,
And in the quiet, hearts intertwine.

Resilience Wrapped in Snow

Winter's breath, a chilling kiss,
Blankets cover every stone.
Yet beneath the icy bliss,
Life endures, steadfast and grown.

Roots hold firm in frozen ground,
Timeless strength in each embrace.
Funds of courage can be found,
Resilience in the quiet space.

Branches bend but do not break,
Beneath the weight of icy life.
Through the trials, hearts awake,
Knowing well the edge of strife.

Nature teaches, slow and wise,
In each flake, a tale is spun.
From the lows to sunny skies,
Every cycle, just begun.

So when the storms of life descend,
Embrace the chill, let hope ignite.
In each struggle, we can mend,
Resilience wrapped in purest white.

Hints of Color in Chilly Air

In the gray, a subtle spark,
Hints of color break the gloom.
Crimson berries, bright and stark,
Embolden winter's chilly womb.

Softest gold in morning light,
Leaves a trace on frosty ground.
Each morning brings a pure delight,
As nature's palette spins around.

Wildlife thrives in muted hues,
Tracks reveal a vibrant chase.
In the quiet, life renews,
Painting joy with gentle grace.

Every breath in crisp, fresh air,
Brings a smile to chilled cheeks' glow.
Hints of color here and there,
Shining hope through winter's snow.

So let us wander, hand in hand,
Through the beauty that we find.
In the cold, together stand,
Hints of color, soft and kind.

The Thawing Muse

In the silence of the dawn,
A whisper stirs the frost,
Colors break, a canvas drawn,
Life reclaimed, but not lost.

Melodies from hidden streams,
Awake the dormant dreams,
Nature's breath fills the air,
Inspiring hearts laid bare.

Buds bloom with gentle grace,
Chasing shadows from their place,
Creativity in full flow,
Painting worlds we long to know.

Hope unfurls like morning light,
Chasing away the night,
In every corner, life resides,
As the thaw reveals what hides.

With each note the soul expands,
Crafting visions in our hands,
A symphony that sways and flows,
As the thawing muse bestows.

Crystalline Petals

In gardens where the frost lays still,
Petals shine in icy grace,
Each one holds a secret thrill,
Captured in a delicate space.

The sun's embrace begins to kiss,
Transforming crystals into light,
Nature whispers tales of bliss,
Awakening colors, pure and bright.

Fragile forms in the morning dew,
Reflecting dreams that softly gleam,
Nature's art in every hue,
Inviting all to share the dream.

With every breeze, a dance unfolds,
As petals twirl with winter's song,
Stories within each beauty hold,
In harmony, where we belong.

Crystalline petals, fleeting charms,
Enchanting hearts, they softly sway,
In the garden, nature's arms,
We find our peace, come what may.

Sleeping in the Cold

Beneath the blanket of the frost,
Dreams of warmth do softly sigh,
In slumber deep, not all is lost,
As time drifts by, and shadows lie.

Silent whispers fill the night,
Echoes of the distant sun,
Bundled tight, we feel the bite,
Yet hope within us still has spun.

Nature slumbers, peaceful, calm,
Hibernation wrapped in white,
In every heart, a soothing balm,
Awaiting Spring's return to light.

Cold may reign in stillness deep,
Yet beneath, the pulse remains,
In dreams of warmth, we gently creep,
Filling voids, releasing chains.

Sleeping in the cold we find,
Rest and peace amidst the chill,
In winter's arms, our thoughts unwind,
Awake we'll be, with dreams to thrill.

Veils of White

Softly falls the silent snow,
Draping earth in veils of white,
Quiet moments, whispers low,
As day succumbs to velvet night.

Cloaked in purity we drift,
Each flake holds a tale of old,
Winter's breath, a tender gift,
In its arms, the world is bold.

Footprints mark a fleeting path,
Through the quiet, hearts ignite,
In this beauty, feel the wrath,
Of nature's power, pure and bright.

Veils of white, a scene serene,
Covering all with soft embrace,
In this realm of winter's sheen,
We find solace and find grace.

Amidst the hush, we ponder deep,
What lies beneath this frosted dome,
In stillness, secrets quietly keep,
As nature dreams, we are at home.

The Shiver of Awakening

Morning light peeks through the trees,
Birds awaken with soft melodies.
Chill grips the air, a gentle embrace,
Nature stirs, finding its place.

Frost kisses blades of grass anew,
Dewdrops shimmer, bright and true.
The world unfolds with shivering hues,
As dreams retreat, and life renews.

Branches sway with a whispered breath,
Life's dance begins, ignoring death.
Each moment feels both fresh and old,
A story of warmth in the bitter cold.

Petals open with cautious grace,
A celebration, a warm embrace.
The sun rises, daylight breaks free,
Awakening life in harmony.

Colors bloom in the warming air,
Hope emerges, shedding despair.
In the quiet, a joyful sound,
The shiver of awakening all around.

Fragrant Echoes of Frost

Winter's breath lays a silvery sheet,
Each flake a whisper, soft and sweet.
Branches adorned in delicate lace,
Nature's perfume fills the space.

Crisp air carries scents profound,
Of pine and earth, all around.
Every footstep crunches below,
Fragrant echoes of frost, aglow.

Candles flicker in the frost-kissed night,
Warmth gathers, a welcoming light.
Beneath blankets of shimmering white,
Hearts grow brighter, taking flight.

The moon hangs low, a watchful eye,
Over frosty fields where dreams lie.
Hope drifts softly, a gentle guide,
Through winter's chill, we abide.

Time moves slowly, in this embrace,
Fragrant echoes fill the space.
In every breath, a promise made,
The beauty of winter softly conveyed.

Shadows of Ice and Bloom

Beneath the frost where shadows lie,
Life waits patiently, a silent sigh.
Ice glints softly in morning's light,
As blossoms dream through the cold night.

A dance of dark and vibrant hues,
As winter wanes, spring's hope renews.
Frosty mornings give way to dew,
A canvas waiting, painted anew.

Branches creak under nature's weight,
While colors mingle, love abates.
In shadows cast by the soft moon's glow,
Secrets whisper where rivers flow.

Petals push through the frosted ground,
In that moment, beauty is found.
The cold retreats, as warmth takes flight,
In shadows of ice, we find the light.

Hope persists in every bloom,
A fierce reminder of life's loom.
In the intersection of dark and bright,
Shadows dance into the night.

Winter's Secret Garden

Hidden beneath blankets, soft and white,
Lies a garden, brimming with light.
Whispers of spring lie deep within,
Awaiting the warmth to begin.

Snowflakes fall like gentle sighs,
Covering dreams, where stillness lies.
Every seed rests, wrapped up tight,
In winter's embrace, sheltered from sight.

Branches cradle a heavy load,
Tracing the path where time bestowed.
Among the frost, hope will unfurl,
As petals yearn to dance and twirl.

The hush of winter, a sacred space,
Nourishing life, revealing grace.
In frost-kissed corners, secrets swell,
Stories of spring that time will tell.

Soon the sun will warm the ground,
And laughter will be the only sound.
In winter's garden, peace abides,
Where every longing quietly resides.

Whispers of Ice

In the stillness of the night,
Silent secrets gleam so bright.
Frozen breath upon the air,
Whispers linger everywhere.

Crystals form on willow's grace,
Nature's beauty, cold embrace.
Underneath the silver sky,
Echoes of the winter's sigh.

Glistening frost on empty trees,
Dancing softly with the breeze.
Silent stories softly told,
In the chill, the warmth of cold.

As the stars begin to fade,
Dreams entwined in icy blade.
Frozen moments, clear and fine,
In the night, a world divine.

Wonder wrapped in layers white,
Painting shadows in the light.
Whispers of a world so still,
In the ice, I find my will.

Chilling Fragrance

In the air, a crisp delight,
Winter's breath, the senses bright.
Essence of the frozen earth,
Chilling fragrance speaks of birth.

Frosted petals, white and pure,
Nature's scent, a timeless cure.
Crisp and sharp, the evening's call,
In the silence, I stand tall.

Beneath the moon's soft silver glow,
Whispers in the breezes flow.
Every breath, a crisp reminder,
Of the beauty that grows kinder.

Fragrant memories linger sweet,
In the cold, my heart skips beat.
Frozen blooms beneath the stars,
Chilling fragrance, love's memoirs.

Through the night, the world transforms,
With each breath, serenity warms.
In the chill, I find my place,
In every frost, a soft embrace.

Petals in the Frost

Petals scatter on the ground,
Softly kissed, without a sound.
Wrapped in layers, winter's quilt,
Beauty rests, the world is built.

Colors muted, shades of grey,
In the frost, they quietly lay.
Moments frozen, time stands still,
Nature's art, a quiet thrill.

Delicate, the flowers sigh,
As the chilly winds pass by.
Each petal bears a tale of grace,
In the frost, they find their place.

Underneath the skies so vast,
Whispers of the seasons past.
Even in the cold's embrace,
Life finds beauty, leaves a trace.

Winter's touch, both soft and bold,
Stories of the earth retold.
Petals in the frost remain,
Silent vows in winter's reign.

Resilience in Dormancy

Beneath the ground, a secret sleeps,
Silent whispers, nature keeps.
Roots embrace the winter's chill,
In the dark, there lies a will.

Dormant dreams in layers deep,
Await the sun, their vigil keep.
Strength in stillness, hope restored,
Nature waits, its heart ignored.

Snowflakes blanket every blade,
In this peace, a promise laid.
Through the frost, the world draws near,
Resilience whispers, ever clear.

Life awaits the warming light,
Gathering strength in frostbit night.
With every cycle, calm and true,
Emerging from the cold anew.

In dormancy, the tales unfold,
Of silent battles, brave and bold.
Resilience wrapped in winter's breath,
Life endures beyond the death.

Shadows Dance in Icy Sunbeams

Shadows stretch across the ground,
Whispers of the night abound.
Frigid light, a shimmering trace,
Dancing spirits in this place.

The sun peeks through the ancient trees,
Caressing branches, a gentle breeze.
Flickering hopes in the glow,
Softly urging life to grow.

Frosted leaves in the morning dew,
Nature's art, a splendid view.
Echoes of warmth in the cold,
A tale of courage, brave and bold.

With each ray, the shadows flee,
Revealing all that's meant to be.
In icy beams, we find our song,
Beneath the light, we all belong.

So let the dance of shadows play,
As winter's grip begins to sway.
Embrace the change, let spirits rise,
In icy sunbeams, see the skies.

Blooms Waiting for the Thaw

Beneath the snow, a promise sleeps,
Cloaked in white, the garden weeps.
Whispers of color, soft and sweet,
Dreaming of warmth, the buds repeat.

Each frozen petal, a secret kept,
In silent waits, the earth has wept.
Laughter of spring is drawing near,
Where once was silence, joy will cheer.

Green shoots push through the icy crust,
Nature's miracle, purest trust.
Hope unfurls in radiant hues,
As winter bids its cold adieu.

Buds awake with a gentle sigh,
In the shimmer of the blue sky.
Waiting patiently, they will bloom,
Bringing life to the endless gloom.

Soon the flowers will paint the ground,
In vibrant colors, joy unbound.
Blooms will dance where shadows lay,
As winter softly turns to May.

Starlit Conversations in the Snow

Under the stars, the world is still,
A blanket of white on the winter hill.
Whispers carried on the night air,
Starlit dreams, a moment rare.

Footprints crunch in the silvery glow,
Echoing tales that the night will know.
Each star a witness, glowing bright,
In the quiet, hearts take flight.

The moon hangs low, a silver coin,
Reflecting secrets that we join.
Conversations soft as falling flakes,
In this magic, our spirit wakes.

Beneath the trees, the shadows play,
Creating figures that sway and sway.
In this wonder, we share our dreams,
Among the starlit, swirling themes.

As snowflakes fall, we laugh and sigh,
In winter's embrace, we freely fly.
Starlit conversations, a shared delight,
Binding our hearts in the soothing night.

Hope Cradled in Frost

In the stillness of a frosty morn,
Hope awakens, reborn.
Cradled closely in nature's arms,
Gentle whispers of unseen charms.

The world is wrapped in a silvery shroud,
A quiet peace, soft and proud.
Each breath sharp, a reminder clear,
That warmth and life are drawing near.

Frosted windowpanes display
The beauty of this frozen day.
Inside, we gather, hearts aglow,
As winter's grip begins to slow.

Seeds of promise beneath the frost,
In every pause, what was lost.
The earth prepares for vibrant change,
In hidden places, life will arrange.

Hope cradled in the winter chill,
Awaits the sun, the heart's sweet thrill.
Through layers thick, the warmth ignites,
Whispered dreams in the frosty nights.

Beneath the Ice

Silent whispers in the night,
Frozen rivers hold on tight.
Secrets dwell where shadows creep,
Beneath the ice, the world is steep.

Frosted branches arch and bend,
Nature's beauty, without end.
Crystal patterns, sharp and clear,
Hidden truths that once were dear.

A fragile world, encased in chill,
Time stands still, yet speaks a thrill.
Echoes linger, soft and low,
Beneath the ice, the tales still flow.

The cold reflection, a mirror's face,
Hints of warmth, a warm embrace.
Underneath, life's pulse beats on,
Beneath the ice, the dawn has drawn.

Listen closely, hear the signs,
Nature's clock, with hidden lines.
In this realm, the stillness breeds,
Beneath the ice, a heart still beats.

A Flower's Heart

In the garden, petals fall,
Silent beauty captures all.
Colors dance within the light,
Whispers bloom in soft delight.

Each gentle breeze, a tender sigh,
Underneath the vast blue sky.
Nature's pulse, a rhythmic start,
Listen close—it's a flower's heart.

Sunlight kisses every hue,
Morning dew, a glistening view.
Life unfolds with every part,
Wrapped within a flower's heart.

Seasons change, yet love remains,
In every bud, a joy sustains.
Through the storms, we play our part,
Trust the rhythm of the heart.

So when you walk through floral trails,
Know the stories that each unveils.
Sprouts of hope, in every chart,
Find the magic of a flower's heart.

Silent Gardens of Snow

Blankets soft cover the ground,
In the stillness, peace is found.
Footprints vanish, time stands still,
Silent gardens, winter's will.

Frosted leaves and branches bare,
Nature holds a secret prayer.
Beneath the snow, life waits and knows,
Silent gardens, where beauty grows.

Whispers heard in the quiet air,
Dreams of spring begin to dare.
In this calm, the heart can flow,
In silent gardens wrapped in snow.

Every flake a story told,
In the warmth of memories old.
Waiting for the sun to show,
Silent gardens, draped in snow.

Embrace the hush, the tender night,
Winter's peace, a sacred light.
Magic lingers, soft and slow,
In silent gardens of pure snow.

Cold Sunlight on Petal's Edge

Morning breaks with muted grace,
Cold sunlight warms each fragile face.
Petals glisten, crisp and bright,
Bathed in chill, yet full of light.

A tender glow, a fragile dance,
Nature's touch, a fleeting chance.
Fresh beginnings, hopes will wedge,
In the cold sunlight on petal's edge.

Shadows deepen as day unfolds,
In this moment, beauty holds.
Every drop, a precious pledge,
Reflects the cold sunlight's edge.

Through the frost, resilience glows,
Strength in every bloom that grows.
Life persists, despite the dredge,
In the cold sunlight on petal's edge.

So let us cherish what we see,
In the chill, there's warmth to be.
Embrace the beauty, let it dredge,
Your heart in cold sunlight on petal's edge.

Dreams Wrapped in White

Through the fog a vision shines,
Dreams wrapped in white, soft as lines.
Blankets over fields and trees,
A hush, a pause, a gentle breeze.

Each flake a promise, pure and true,
World transformed in softest hue.
Whispered secrets, nothing contrives,
Dreams wrapped in white, our hope survives.

In this quiet, the heart finds peace,
From the chaos, a sweet release.
Winter's magic, a calming tide,
Cradling dreams where we reside.

Glowing softly, the moonlight streams,
Illuminating all our dreams.
In gentle folds, like love's own site,
Nestled safely, wrapped in white.

So hold these moments, sweet and bright,
Embrace the calm of winter's night.
Each dream a star that takes its flight,
As life unfolds, wrapped in white.

The Heart of the Cold

In shadows deep where silence grows,
The heart of winter gently glows.
With icy breath, the whispers call,
Each flake a dream that starts to fall.

The trees stand bare, their branches weave,
A tapestry that time believes.
And through the nights, the stars are bright,
They pierce the cold with silver light.

A frozen stream, a mirror's grace,
Reflecting stillness in this place.
Each step on snow, a gentle sound,
Where peace and solitude are found.

Yet under frost, the life persists,
In hidden roots and hopeful twists.
The heart awakens when the thaw
Will break the chains with nature's law.

So in this cold, we find our way,
Through winter's night towards the day.
Embrace the chill, for in it lies,
A promise born beneath the skies.

Changes in the Chill

In morning light, the frost appears,
Transforming whispers into cheers.
The world adorned in sparkling white,
A canvas fresh with pure delight.

Amidst the still, the branches sway,
The chill reveals, in subtle way.
Each breath a cloud, a sigh of dreams,
A spark ignites in winter's gleams.

Yet time will shift, and warmth will breathe,
The chill retreats, as life believes.
The earth will thaw with colors bright,
In changing tides, we find our light.

For every frost, there lies a hint,
Of blossoms born from winter's print.
A dance of seasons, young and old,
In every change, a tale is told.

So cherish now this fleeting bite,
Embrace the chill, the fleeting light.
For soon the bloom will praise the sun,
And in that shift, new life begun.

Cradle of the Frost

In a cradle soft, the frost will lay,
A blanket pure that keeps at bay.
The tender shoots, they hide and dream,
In sleep, they wait for spring's warm beam.

With gentle hands, the cold will hold,
Embracing life, both shy and bold.
A hush envelops earth and sky,
Where whispers dance and time goes by.

Each crystal shines, a fleeting spark,
A memory lost, a lover's mark.
And in this quiet, magic brews,
In frost's embrace, we find our muse.

The moonlight bathes the world in glows,
As nature sings in frozen prose.
The cradle rocks with ancient lore,
A silent song we can't ignore.

So let us pause, in wonder stand,
And feel the chill, the frosty hand.
For in this cradle, stories start,
Of life reborn, and nature's art.

Echoes of a Frozen Garden

In a garden hushed beneath the snow,
The echoes of the past still flow.
Each petal's ghost in silence sighs,
A memory held where beauty lies.

The pathways dressed in icy lace,
Where life awaits to find its space.
In stillness vast, a tale unfolds,
Of seasons' change and whispers bold.

Yet deep below, the roots remain,
In frozen earth, their dreams sustain.
A heartbeat lies in slumber deep,
In nature's arms, they gently sleep.

With every thaw, the colors rise,
A symphony beneath the skies.
The garden wakes, a vibrant song,
Where echoes of the past belong.

So let us wander, hand in hand,
Through echoes of this frozen land.
For in each step, the promise grows,
Of life reborn where beauty flows.

The Season's Gentle Exhale

Leaves whisper soft, a final sigh,
Nature's lullaby beneath the sky.
Fields once vibrant, now fade to brown,
As autumn's breath sweeps through the town.

Cool winds carry stories untold,
Each branch now bare, a sight to behold.
Chasing shadows as daylight wanes,
The season's beauty in quiet frames.

Flickering fires warm the night,
Embers glowing, a comforting light.
Hot cider steaming, aromas sweet,
Gathered together, hearts feel complete.

Stars emerge in the velvet dark,
A canvas painted with nature's spark.
Resting dreams in a tranquil space,
The gentle exhale, a warm embrace.

Chilled Beauty in Quiet Corners

Snowflakes dance, a silent swirl,
Each unique form, a magical pearl.
Blankets of white wrap the earth tight,
In corners where stillness greets the night.

Icicles glisten, nature's art,
Hanging like jewels, a frosty heart.
Brittle whispers in shadows play,
As winter's chill holds the world at bay.

Crimson branches pierce the gray,
Hints of warmth in the cold's ballet.
Footprints trace stories in the snow,
In quiet corners, life feels slow.

The world breathes deep, a frozen time,
Nature's pulse, an unspoken rhyme.
In every drift, a tale untold,
Chilled beauty shining, brave and bold.

Frosted Silence

Morning breaks, a crystal glow,
Frosted silence blankets below.
Each breath visible in the air,
The stillness whispers, pure and rare.

Trees stand tall in white adorned,
Nature's canvas, softly formed.
Gentle hues of blue and gray,
In frosted silence, dreams drift away.

Time feels slow in the heart of dawn,
Where beauty lingers and hope is drawn.
Nature's secrets, wrapped in mist,
In this hush, we find what we've missed.

Echoes faint in the chilly breeze,
Memories dance among the trees.
Each moment captured, fleeting yet vast,
In frosted silence, we hold it fast.

Hidden Colors

Beneath the frost, a story lies,
Hidden colors, nature's surprise.
Emerging slowly as daylight grows,
Life awakens beneath the snows.

Lush greens fight through winter's grip,
Bursting forth on slender tips.
Petals shy in the morning light,
Whispers of life put up a fight.

Moss-covered stones, a vibrant hue,
Nature's palette, ever true.
In forgotten corners, beauty breathes,
Hidden colors in winter's eaves.

Each shade tells of tales unseen,
The warmth of spring, the sadness keen.
In the quiet, the world prepares,
For blossoms waiting, love declares.

Evergreen Fragments in a Crystal World

Amidst the frost, green fragments stand,
Evergreen life in a crystal land.
Symbols of hope in winter's clutch,
Holding on, they matter much.

Needles glisten with icy tears,
Whispering tales of forgotten years.
Roots dig deep, through the cold they fight,
Evergreen strength is a wondrous sight.

Branches sway in the biting breeze,
Guardians of whispers, of ancient trees.
Their spirit gleams as the seasons shift,
In a world of crystal, they are a gift.

Nature's promise wrapped in green,
Everlasting beauty, yet unseen.
Through winter's grasp, resilience thrives,
In evergreen fragments, the world revives.

The Quiet Awakening

In dawn's soft glow, dreams take flight,
The world in hush, bathed in light.
Whispers of hope in the morning air,
A gentle call, as souls prepare.

Nature stirs, with a tender sigh,
Buds begin to reach for the sky.
Every heartbeat, a story untold,
In the warmth of the sun, life unfolds.

Silent whispers, the trees stand tall,
Promises echo, in nature's hall.
Together, they dance in the breeze,
Awakening softly, with such ease.

Rays of gold through branches weave,
A symphony, the heart believes.
With every moment, new dreams arise,
In the quiet, we realize.

So here we pause, breathe in the day,
Embracing life in every way.
For in this stillness, we find our way,
Into the dawn of a brand new day.

Icy Vows

Beneath the frost, love's whispers tread,
Promises lingering, words unsaid.
In the chill of night, hearts intertwined,
Frozen in time, together aligned.

Crystals gleam on branches, so rare,
Each flake a vow, a silent prayer.
In the cold, we find warmth's embrace,
A flicker of hope in the frigid space.

Bitter winds may howl and bite,
Yet in your eyes, I find the light.
Amidst the ice, our passion stays,
In every heartbeat, love displays.

Winter's grasp, a test of time,
Yet with you, I feel sublime.
Hand in hand, we brave the storm,
Through icy paths, hearts stay warm.

When spring arrives, the snow will fade,
Yet our vows shall never trade.
For in the frost, I found my truth,
In icy bonds, we live our youth.

Shivering Beauty

Upon the hill, the flowers bend,
A glimpse of grace, nature's friend.
Understated, in colors few,
Shivering beauty, fresh and new.

Petals quiver with the breeze,
Dancing softly with such ease.
A fleeting moment, so divine,
Captured in the morning's shine.

The dew drops glisten, a crystal crown,
Adorning blossoms of rich renown.
In stillness, they tell tales untold,
Of petals' dreams in shades of gold.

Time whispers by, but beauty stays,
In a world of fleeting days.
Each moment still, yet so alive,
In the art of nature, we thrive.

So let us cherish this simple sight,
These fragile blooms, a pure delight.
In every shiver, a song we hum,
In nature's arms, our hearts succumb.

Hibernating Hues

In the depths of winter's embrace,
Colors await their time and place.
Under layers, they softly sleep,
Dreaming of spring, in silence deep.

Muted tones in the quiet white,
Whispers of life hidden from sight.
A canvas blank, yet full of dreams,
Waiting for warmth, the sunbeam's gleam.

Each shaded hue, a story kept,
In hibernation, secrets swept.
Nature's palette, resting still,
Gathering strength for the coming thrill.

When the thaw breaks, colors will blaze,
Painting the world in vibrant ways.
But for now, they conserve their grace,
In slumber soft, a tender space.

So let us wait for the colors to rise,
From winter's clutch, beneath grey skies.
For in hibernation, we find our muse,
In nature's cycle, hibernating hues.

Frozen Whispers of Renewed Growth

In shadows deep, where silence breathes,
Dreams lie still beneath the leaves.
Winter's cloak holds secrets tight,
Awaiting dawn, the softest light.

Beneath the snow, the roots embrace,
Quiet murmurs of a hidden place.
Life stirs gently, not far away,
Whispers of growth, at break of day.

The frost may bite, but hearts remain,
Hoping for warmth, despite the pain.
Each frozen tear, a precious gem,
A promise kept, in nature's hem.

As sunbeams break the icy chains,
Softly melting away the pains.
In every breath, a song of grace,
Renewal waits, in time and space.

So listen close, to whispers low,
In frozen realms, the secrets grow.
With patience held and faith in sight,
The world will bloom, from dark to light.

Snow-Covered Hues

Blankets white drape fields anew,
Covering flaws in a shimmering hue.
Each flake dances, a gentle fall,
A quiet magic, enchanting all.

Footprints whisper through the chill,
Silent echoes, the world stands still.
Each breath a cloud, a frosty lace,
In winter's arms, we find our place.

Trees wear crowns of glistening frost,
A fleeting moment, never lost.
Beneath the calm, a heartbeat glows,
In snow-covered dreams, anything goes.

As daylight wanes, twilight unfolds,
A canvas painted in blues and golds.
The evening wraps its velvet glow,
In this serene, enchanted show.

So cherish each snow-covered sight,
A fleeting dream, but pure delight.
For every layer that nature weaves,
A tapestry of hope believes.

A Secret Song

In quiet woods where shadows dwell,
A melody soft, a gentle spell.
Leaves rustle with a whispered tune,
Nature's heart beats beneath the moon.

Birds join in with a serenade,
Notes flowing through the summer glade.
Each sound weaves through branches high,
A secret song that fills the sky.

Streams babble with a playful cheer,
Echoing stories for all to hear.
In every note, the world awakens,
A heart in tune, no sound mistaken.

Beneath the stars, where dreams unite,
The secret song hums through the night.
In every breath, a story sung,
Of fleeting times when we were young.

So listen close to the whispers near,
In nature's choir, find joy and cheer.
For every heartbeat, every throng,
Is part of life's unending song.

Petals Cautiously Unfurling

With early light, the garden wakes,
A tender grace, the softly breaks.
Petals shy, begin to show,
In colors bright, a gentle glow.

Each bud a promise, held so tight,
Cautious beauty, in morning light.
The air is sweet with fragrant dreams,
In whispered hope, the sun's warm beams.

Soft winds kiss the fragile blooms,
Dancing light through leafy rooms.
Nature's sigh, a soothing balm,
In this moment, all feels calm.

Every petal tells a tale,
Of sun and rain, a vibrant scale.
With patience drawn, they fully spread,
In blooms of life, joy is bred.

So watch the garden, day by day,
As beauty finds its boldest way.
For in each flower that dares to rise,
Lies the magic of the skies.

Waiting for the Warmth

In chilly air, the world awaits,
A pause of hope that love creates.
Frosty mornings hold dreams inside,
As nature waits with arms spread wide.

Buds hold secrets, wrapped in chill,
With every breath, they yearn to fill.
The sun will grant a tender kiss,
To break the cold with warmth and bliss.

Patience, the song that nature sings,
In quiet moments, the future springs.
Each day draws near to brighter days,
A longing heart finds myriad ways.

The earth holds tight to whispered tales,
Of summers past and gentle gales.
In every inch, a story swells,
Of warmth returning as time compels.

So wait awhile, for joy to bloom,
In every heart, dispelling gloom.
For warmth will come, as sure as breath,
To paint our world, beyond the death.

A Silent Promise

In the stillness of the night,
Stars are whispering soft and bright.
In each gleam, a bond we share,
A silent promise floating in air.

Mountains hold their ancient grace,
In their shadows, we find our place.
Every peak tells tales untold,
Of dreams fulfilled and hearts made bold.

Waves lap softly on the shore,
Each swell echoes, a distant roar.
In the rhythm, a vow so deep,
Awakening treasures we seek to keep.

The moon's glow casts a tender light,
Guiding paths through endless night.
In each heartbeat, the promise stays,
A silent vow that never decays.

So hold this truth, let it ignite,
In every shadow, find the light.
For life's great dance, in cosmic rhyme,
Is a silent promise, through all time.

www.ingramcontent.com/pod-product-compliance
Ingram Content Group UK Ltd.
Pitfield, Milton Keynes, MK11 3LW, UK
UKHW031954131224
452403UK00010B/580

9 789916 799918